T0286793

Cambridge Elements ≡

Public Economics
edited by
Robin Boadway
Queen's University
Frank A. Cowell
The London School of Economics and Political Science
and
Massimo Florio
University of Milan

WELFARE STATES: ACHIEVEMENTS AND THREATS

Peter H. Lindert
University of California, Davis

CAMBRIDGE
UNIVERSITY PRESS

CAMBRIDGE
UNIVERSITY PRESS

University Printing House, Cambridge CB2 8BS, United Kingdom

One Liberty Plaza, 20th Floor, New York, NY 10006, USA

477 Williamstown Road, Port Melbourne, VIC 3207, Australia

314–321, 3rd Floor, Plot 3, Splendor Forum, Jasola District Centre,
New Delhi – 110025, India

79 Anson Road, #06–04/06, Singapore 079906

Cambridge University Press is part of the University of Cambridge.

It furthers the University's mission by disseminating knowledge in the pursuit of
education, learning, and research at the highest international levels of excellence.

www.cambridge.org
Information on this title: www.cambridge.org/9781108464338
DOI: 10.1017/9781108565431

First published 2019

A catalogue record for this publication is available from the British Library.

ISBN 978-1-108-46433-8 Paperback
ISSN 2516-2276 (online)
ISSN 2516-2268 (print)

Welfare States

Achievements and Threats

Elements in Public Economics

DOI: 10.1017/9781108565431
First published online: December 2018

Peter H. Lindert
University of California – Davis and NBER

Abstract: The traditionally, and wrongly, imagined vulnerabilities of the welfare state are economic. The true threats are demographic and political.

The most frequently imagined threat is that the welfare-state package reduces the level and growth of GDP. It does not, according to broad historical patterns and non-experimental panel econometrics. Large-budget welfare states achieve a host of social improvements without any clear loss of GDP. This Element elaborates on how this "free lunch" is gained in practice.

Other threats to the welfare state are more real, however. Two demographic-political clouds loom on the horizon in the twenty-first century, though neither cloud reveals an economic flaw specific to the welfare state. One cloud is the rise of anti-immigrant backlash. If combined with heavy refugee inflows, this could destroy future public support for universalist welfare-state programs, even though they seem to remain economically sound. The other, and more certainly rain-bearing, cloud is that population aging poses a serious problem for financing old age, either publicly or privately. Pension deficits threaten to crowd out more productive social spending. Only a few countries have faced this issue very well.

Keywords: social spending, welfare state, fiscal redistribution, economic history, public pensions

ISBNs 9781108464338 (PB) 9781108565431 (OC)
ISSNs 2516-2276 (online) 2516-2268 (print)

Contents

1 The Big Picture

1.1 Theories about Economic Effects

Economists approach the subject of the welfare state with the characteristic two-handed approach that so famously annoyed President Truman. On the one hand, social insurance against income shocks theoretically provides the same kinds of benefits as private insurance. And government might theoretically do it better. Consumption smoothing across states of the world might possibly be achieved better through government funding and provision when private insurance markets fail to solve the problems of asymmetric information and adverse selection, especially in health insurance. In addition, the very progressivity of tax-based social insurance may serve popular preferences for more equal aggregate outcomes. Government social insurance might also reap economies of scale more efficiently than competing private firms.

On the other hand, suspicions run deep about possible anti-growth incentive effects. People's incentives to engage in productive behavior might be reduced by taxing behavior and handing assistance to those who behave unproductively. Governments can also be susceptible to corruption, and to inefficiencies caused by the lack of competition and Parkinsonian empire-building.

This essay is organized around examining the negative possibilities, noting the positive achievements of the welfare state only *en passant*. It first reviews the evidence on the imagined anti-growth economic effects of the welfare state over the last hundred years, and then weighs which negative possibilities do or do not loom between now and mid-century. The evidence seems to say that the traditionally imagined economic flaws of the welfare state do not show up in practice, and pose no clear threat to the welfare state anytime soon. The welfare state has achieved great income stability, lower inequality, lower poverty rates, and longer life without significantly reducing GDP or employment. The true threats are demographic and political, not economic.

1.2 A Preview of Verdicts

Since World War II, about a dozen rich countries have channeled more than a fifth of national product into social transfers, and about a quarter of national product if we include public education as part of social spending.[1] Those

---

[1] This paper defines "social transfers" as taxpayer-funded government expenditures on health care, pensions, family assistance (Americans' "welfare"), unemployment compensation, active labor-market spending (retraining, etc.), and public housing subsidies. My definition of social transfers nearly matches the official OECD definition of "public social expenditure." The main difference between the two is that I would, whenever the data permit, exclude the pension benefits paid to public employees. These are part of a labor contract, comparable to private labor contracts, and

countries, in order of their social transfer share of GDP in the first decade of this century, are France, Sweden, Austria, Belgium, Denmark, Germany, Finland, Italy, Portugal, and Spain, with Norway, the Netherlands, and the United Kingdom near the margin. Contrasting their experience with that of other countries provides a historical test case for the effects of tax-based social spending. That historical case seems to have delivered these five clear verdicts:

(1) One imagined threat rejected by the historical facts is the widespread suspicion that the welfare-state package reduces the level and growth of GDP. Global history does not show any clear overall negative effect of larger tax-financed social transfers on national product. The widespread belief in large GDP costs of the high-budget welfare state is based on theory and inappropriate tests. The real world never ran the kinds of experiments that so many have chosen to imagine. The best available statistical tests underline a "free lunch puzzle": Europe's large tax-based social budgets have apparently not lowered GDP, as documented below.

(2) That "free lunch" has delivered several fundamental human gains reaped by large welfare states. The larger welfare states have achieved lower income inequality, lower gender inequality, lower poverty rates, and longer life, again without any clear loss in GDP. Nor do they suffer any other often-imagined side effects. The large welfare states, particularly in Northern Europe, have some of the world's cleanest and least corrupt governments, with lower budget deficits than the United States, Japan, and other rich countries. And, for what it is worth, their populations express greater happiness in international surveys of public opinion.

(3) What made that possible? The "free lunch puzzle" of the welfare state is easily understood when one examines how actual practice has evolved. Both sides of the Atlantic have made some mistakes when trying to draw an efficient border between governments and markets. The main mistakes on the American side relate to insufficient anti-poverty programs,

---

not redistributions from the rest of society. OECD allowed such a separation in its social expenditure series for 1960–1981, but not for its current series starting in 1980.

I define "social expenditures" as these social transfers plus public spending on education. This broader definition matches the definition used by Garfinkel, Rainwater, and Smeeding (2010).

My arbitrary definition of the "welfare state" is any democratic country for which social transfers, and the taxes implicitly paying for them, exceed 20 percent of GDP. Had I defined the welfare state as any country devoting more than 20 percent of GDP to social spending, including public education spending à la Garfinkel et al. (2010), it would have been easier to show (as they do) that the welfare state is not bad for economic growth. For rhetorical purposes, I prefer the more stringent test focusing on social *transfers*, which are more controversial, and less obviously productive, than public expenditures on education, which I separate from my discussion of the "welfare state."

inefficient health insurance, underinvestment in mothers' careers, and the under-taxation of addictive goods (tobacco, alcohol, and gasoline).

(4) The main longer-run institutional mistakes in Mediterranean Europe relate to excessive protection of vested interests against competition in product and labor markets, not the welfare state. As for the economic crisis starting 2007, which started in the United States, neither its timing nor its location relates to the welfare state as such. The main causes of crisis in the not-so-welfare-state Mediterranean and Ireland since 2007 have been the real estate bubble, under-regulation of finance, and Greece's flawed public budgeting.

(4) Other threats to the welfare state are more real, however. One can see two demographic-political clouds on the horizon in the twenty-first century, though neither reveals an economic flaw specific to the welfare state. The first cloud is the rise of anti-immigrant backlash. This could destroy future public support for universalist welfare-state programs, even though they seem to remain economically sound. Such a retreat from the welfare state is a threat mainly to Sweden and Germany, i.e. to those welfare states that continue admitting large permanent refugee inflows while refusing to discriminate against immigrants in providing social services.

(5) A second cloud, larger and more global, is that the rapid acceleration of population aging poses a serious problem for financing old age, either publicly or privately. Only a few countries have addressed this issue with major reforms so far.

The general mission drift in social policy, away from immigrants and toward the elderly, threatens to undermine social investment in children, especially in poor children. Even with the same share of social budgets in future GDP, progressivity and human-capital growth may erode.

The remainder of this paper summarizes the evidence regarding these five verdicts. We turn first to the traditionally, and wrongly, imagined threat related to the welfare state, and then to the two real threats.

2 An Imagined Threat: Isn't the Welfare State Bad for Growth?

If having generous social insurance programs reduces the level and growth of GDP, then sooner or later this negative effect should cause a decline of the welfare state. Such a fear underlies the many books and articles written in the late twentieth century about the "crisis" and "demise" of the welfare state – that is, about an event that has still not happened.

The defense of public social spending and the welfare state rests on quantitative tests that are abundant – and individually non-persuasive.

An economist would prefer a quasi-experimental structural identification using powerful instruments that pass strong tests of exogeneity. The path to this goal is blocked by the fact that each observation must be a whole polity, usually a national government, for each time period. In the absence of credibly randomized data sets of sufficient size, we must retreat to three kinds of contaminated evidence on this imagined threat: sheer survival of the welfare state; raw correlations between social spending and GDP, or GDP growth; and tests that pool international experience without firmly establishing structural determinants.

2.1 A Simple Survival Test

Perhaps the simplest clue about the relationship of tax-based social spending to economic growth lies in a straightforward survival test of the sort George Stigler favored in the field of industrial organization. The survival test has the attraction of avoiding the need to identify causal structure. In a complex multivariate world, one can simply view the resulting health outcome, say for a type of firm or a type of government, by seeing if that type survived. Any type that contained a major inherent flaw would go out of existence.

The survival results are easily summarized. Two hundred years ago, only a handful of national governments spent anything on social transfers, and no government spent as much as 3 percent of GDP on them. Today, at least 164 national governments have positive safety-net transfers, according to World Bank and IMF data. About seventeen rich OECD countries qualify as welfare states, by transferring at least 20 percent of GDP.

Nor has there been any retreat from high social budgets since around 1980, when Margaret Thatcher, Ronald Reagan, and others launched an all-out attack on the welfare state. From 1980 to the cyclical peak of 2007, only one country out of the twenty-three core OECD countries cut the share of GDP transferred to the poor, the sick, and the elderly. Even in that one case, the Netherlands, the drop from 23.3 percent of GDP in 1980 to 19.9 percent of GDP in the cyclical peak of 2007 was nearly canceled by 2013, when government transferred 22.9 percent of GDP. Social safety-net programs, and the welfare state that uses them so heavily, appear to be Darwinian survivors.

2.2 Correlating Social Budgets and GDP: The "Free-Lunch Puzzle"

Similarly, history shows no correlations pitting the welfare state against growth. For at least three centuries, many have insisted that taxed-based social spending cuts jobs and output. So strident is the opposition that one would

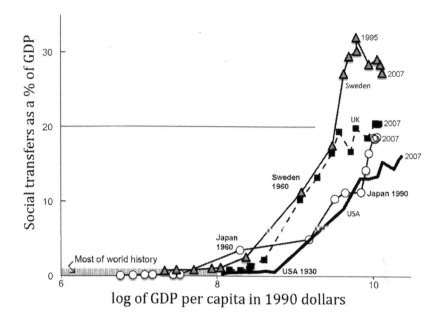

Figure 1 The welfare state is young and rich

The real GDP per capita series up to 2007 is from the Angus Maddison internet site: www.worldeconomics.com/Data/MadisonHistoricalGDP/Madison% 20Historical%20GDP%20Data.efp. The social transfer shares of GDP on the vertical axis for 1880–1930 are from Lindert (1994), and those for 1960–2007 are from the OECD's SOCX series downloadable from OECD iLibrary.

expect it to have resulted from looking directly at some glaring evidence from history. If the negative effects of welfare-state programs were so clear, then perhaps even the raw data should have shown it on a huge IMAX screen.

No such glaring evidence has ever appeared. An obvious starting point would be to glance at the broad sweep of the history of national product, which should have been lower where tax-based social spending was higher. The glance, however, yields the big-screen evidence shown in Figure 1. Most of world history has languished in the lower left-hand corner, with poverty and no social help to the poor, the sick, or the elderly. This is the dreary world that Adam Smith called "barbarous."[2] In the two and a half centuries since Smith wrote, a few dozen countries have taken off into prosperity, as illustrated in Figure 1 by four countries that Smith would have called "civilized" – the United Kingdom, the United States, Sweden, and Japan. While prospering,

---

[2] "There are many expences necessary in a civilized country for which there is no occasion in one that is barbarous." Smith (1766), pp. 530–531.

Table 1 How social transfers as a share of GDP correlate with
growth and prosperity in 19 OECD Countries, 1880–2000
The coefficient of correlation between the initial share of social
transfers in GDP and

Time period	(a) the growth of GDP/capita	(b) the level of GDP/capita
1880–1890	0.10	−0.18
1890–1900	0.34	−0.05
1900–1910	−0.23	0.09
1910–1920	0.12	0.31
1920–1930	−0.24	0.49
1960–1970	−0.16	−0.24
1970–1980	0.34	−0.09
1980–1990	−0.07	0.09
1990–2000	−0.11	−0.04
2000–2010	0.12	−0.19
Simple average of these correlations	0.02	0.02

None of the correlations is statistically significant.
Social transfers/GDP for 1880–1930: Welfare, unemployment, pensions,
health, and housing subsidies, as given in Lindert (1994, table 1).
Social transfers/GDP for 1960–1980: OECD old series (OECD 1985);
1980–present: OECD new series (OECD iLibrary).
Real GDP per capita: Penn World Table 7.1, downloaded 1 April 2013.
The 19 countries are Australia, Austria, Belgium, Canada, Denmark,
Finland, France, Germany, Greece (1960s on), Ireland (1960s on), Italy,
Japan, the Netherlands, New Zealand, Norway, Sweden, Switzerland, the
United Kingdom, and the United States.

they also channeled a greater and greater share of their national product into
taxes spent on social programs. Yet they continued to prosper. One who
believes that the social programs destroy initiative and progress might claim
reserve causation: perhaps it is the prosperity that bred the wasteful social
spending. Yet if the social spending is nothing but a rich country's bad habit,
like obesity or recreational drugs, why don't we see any easy evidence of its
dragging down GDP per person?

One would rightly demand a closer look than this glance at the broad screen.
Sticking to raw correlations for the moment, we may ask whether looking at all
countries and over shorter periods of time shows a negative relationship
between their growth experiences and their use of welfare state expenditures.
Table 1 shows the results for as many decades (ten) and as many countries

(nineteen) as provide systematic long-term data. As reported there, history again provides no significantly negative relationship between the start-of-decade social spending share and either the growth or the level of GDP per person. If we had included the many poorer countries that failed to report social spending because they had little or none of it, there would be more chance of a positive correlation across history, as Figure 1 has already hinted. We cannot infer from all these correlations any positive causal influence of social spending on economic growth. Still, any claim of a negative historical relationship is even easier to doubt.

Within nations, as well as between them, we find no secure negative correlation between local governments' social transfers and either the level or growth of product per capita. For all the anecdotes about companies fleeing high-tax states for low-tax states, there is no net result showing any damage to the higher-taxing and higher-welfare localities. The only time that the anti-government Southern states in the United States rose toward the national average income per capita was in the period 1940–1973 when the South reaped disproportionate benefits from government military and aerospace spending. Such spending not only created jobs and income within the South, but it also raised Southern pay rates by attracting Southern workers to Northern and Pacific Coast cities. Since the rise of welfare payments and other social spending in the 1960s and 1970s, there has been no erosion in the relative incomes or realty values of such larger-transfer states as Connecticut and California. There is no outward evidence of massive tax flight, no "race to the bottom."

2.3 Not-so-Structural Econometrics with International Pools

One should, of course, go deeper, if possible, into statistical tests that really hold other things equal. We know well that both social transfers and national product have many separate, though overlapping, causal determinants. Surely social spending is not just the result of being a rich country, and a country's prosperity depends on many more things than just social spending and the incentives it may create.

Since around 1990, economists have poured great effort into developing truly randomized trials, like those now proliferating in medical science. These are statistically superior to testing from historical experience, since the randomly selected treatment group of observations is subject to influences clearly not experienced by the control group. Yet as warned above, the history of entire nations is not a randomized trial. It does not offer a treatment group of dozens of societies that were beset by welfare-state policies imposed on them by completely outside forces, forces not experienced by a large control group of otherwise similar societies. A few econometric studies have been lucky enough to find "natural experiments," in which history imitates the random-trial laboratory. Yet for large complex forces like the welfare state, no such randomized historical experiment is available.

Lacking truly random trials, economists are forced to extract what causal insights they can from a messy panel of human experiences over time and space, a panel in which both the determinants of social spending and the determinants of GDP might be disentangled even though they overlap and are confounded by a host of other forces. Almost none of the econometric studies published since the 1980s has found a significant negative effect of the whole welfare-state package on GDP.[3] Even the few that announced negative effects, without making their data public, have failed to show negative effects large enough to imply the major economic damage imagined by some theorists, journalists, and politicians.

The lack of clearly negative effects of tax-based social transfers on the level and growth of GDP is all the more remarkable because the tests typically hobble the welfare state variables with two devices that should have shown a negative effect. The first is a handicap that this author has also adopted, in order to toughen the test: exclude public spending on education from the "welfare state" bundle. Public expenditures on education have such clearly positive effects that omitting them raises the odds of finding against the welfare state.[4] Second, all the tests on historical time–space panels hobble the welfare state with a reverse-causation bias. Safety net programs, such as family assistance or unemployment compensation, are designed so that they pay out more when GDP and jobs have slumped – and pay out less when the economy improves. Thus transfer spending will appear guilty of causing slumps, and cutting that spending will be credited with causing the recovery, unless one somehow perfectly identifies the macro-economic shocks causing any movement in GDP. The false guilt is analogous to blaming hospitals for causing deaths because so many people die there.[5] Given these two handicaps, it is all

---

[3] See Landau (1985), Korpi (1985), McCallum and Blais (1987), Castle and Dowrick (1990), Weede (1991), Easterly and Rebelo (1993), Hansson and Henrekson (1994), Persson and Tabellini (1994), Commander, Davoodi, and Lee (1997), Mendoza, Milesi-Ferretti, and Asea (1997), Fölster and Henrekson (1998), Agell, Lindh, and Ohlsson (1999), Kneller, Bleaney, and Gemmell (1999) and by Gemmell, Kneller, and Sanz (2011). For a comparison and summary of all of the late-twentieth-century studies, see Lindert (2004, chapters 10 and 18, especially table 18.1). For a new summary and more recent evidence, see Bakija et al. (2016, chapters 2 and 3).

[4] For a review of rates of economic return on education around the world, see Psacharapoulos and Patrinos (2004a, 2004b), and also the earlier studies cited there.

[5] This second bias shows up even in the set of econometric panel tests that seems the best candidate for an objective discovery of negative growth effects. Overlapping studies by Kneller, Bleaney, and Gemmell (1999) and by Gemmell, Kneller, and Sanz (2011). The authors did not put any weight on the negative result about social spending, but that negative implication from their study should be taken seriously. With their help, I have found that even their best-practice

the more remarkable that social transfers and other measures of the welfare state do not show clearly negative effects on jobs or growth.

While not paying any clear net cost in terms of GDP, the large welfare states seem to have achieved many other things with their social transfers.[6] Here is a quick list of social goals they have served at least as well as other rich countries on the average:

(1) They have consistently enjoyed a more equal distribution of incomes.[7]
(2) They have lower shares of their population in poverty, whether the poverty line is defined as a share of median income or as an absolute level of consumption per person.[8]
(3) The welfare states tend to have longer life expectancy than other OECD countries at similar income levels. How this might relate to public health care is reviewed in Section 3.
(4) The welfare states have some of the world's cleanest and least corrupt governments, despite what some might have predicted from the large amounts passing through government hands.[9]
(5) Welfare states do not run larger budget deficits. There is no correlation at all between the GDP shares of social transfers and the net budget deficit.[10]

---

econometric test has trouble identifying the shocks that we know were there, given our reading of recent history. For example, we know that at the start of the 1990s, Finland suffered a major macro-shock from the collapse of its main trading partner (the Soviet Union) and from mistakenly keeping the Finnish Mark pegged to the soaring German Mark. Yet these authors' tests have no way of picking up such idiosyncratic large macro-shocks that are neither time-fixed effects for all countries nor fixed country effects for all times. The result is a misleading correlation between Finland's huge safety net expenditures and the plummeting of Finland's GDP. I thank Richard Kneller for making their underlying data set available.

[6] Here is a rough quantification of the points listed in this section. Data from twenty-three countries circa 2007 show that the share of social transfers in GDP, our welfare-state indicator, has these correlations with social achievements: (a) a negative 0.56 with the share of households having less than 40 percent of median household income; (b) $^{+}0.39$ with life expectancy, (c) $^{+}0.21$ with Transparency International's clean government indicator, and (d) no overall correlation (0.01) with government budget surplus in 2007–2009. Correlations (a) through (c) were statistically significant at the 5 percent level. The sources are those cited elsewhere in this section.

[7] See Wang et al. (2012) on OECD countries' inequality in 2004, and Lindert (2017) on pre-fisc and post-fisc inequality in fifty-three countries circa 2013. For a readable and balanced summary of the definition of equality in terms of "vertical equity" and the case for progressivity in redistribution, see Slemrod and Bakija (2004), especially chapter 3.

[8] On the poverty shares relative to median incomes, see OECD, Growing Unequal (2008, p. 127). International comparisons of absolute poverty are found in studies by the Luxembourg Income Study; see Smeeding (2006), and Scruggs and Allan (2005).

[9] For Transparency International's index of clean government, called its "Corruption Perceptions Index," www.infoplease.com/world/statistics/2007-transparency-international-corruption-perceptions.html .

[10] On government budget surpluses as shares of GDP, 2007 and 2009, see IMF eLibrary.

(6) Finally, for what they are worth, international polls of public opinion find high average expressions of personal happiness in the high-spending welfare states.[11]

3 Some Reasons Why Growth Hasn't Suffered

What has made this possible? How could the large welfare states have avoided any of the imagined net cost in terms of GDP, while making progress on so many social concerns? A balanced tentative answer seems to be that the few ways in which large tax-based social transfer programs reduce GDP are balanced by ways in which they raise GDP. The heaviest weight on the negative side of the scales seems to be unemployment compensation. Even allowing for some statistical biases against such programs, the empirical literature seems to say that more generous unemployment compensation does indeed reduce jobs and output somewhat. This negative effect, however, is offset by several GDP-enhancing effects of the way in which the welfare state has worked in practice. We turn next to three such effects.

3.1 A More Efficient Tax and Transfer Mix

While a critic might choose to imagine a foolish hypothetical welfare state riddled with bureaucracy, initiative-discouraging taxes, and transfers that subsidize a lifetime of laziness, no such fiscal system has ever prevailed in a welfare state. On the contrary, real-world welfare states have features that make their tax-based social programs less bureaucratic, less expensive in administrative terms, and less in conflict with economic theory than many have imagined.

One such feature is that universalism is efficient on the expenditure side. Universalist expenditure programs, to which everybody is entitled, are cheaper to administer because there is less bureaucratic need to investigate who should be excluded from the benefits.[12]

In the case of health insurance and health care, for example, comparative studies have consistently found that administrative costs are a lower share of the health care delivery expenditures in the more public programs of Canada and Europe.[13] Universalist public insurance and public provision is less

---

[11] On international differences in expressions of happiness, see the World Values Survey; e.g. www.nationmaster.com/graph/lif_hap_net-lifestyle-happiness-net.

[12] For a general discussion of this point, see Lindert (2004, chapters 4, 10, and 12) and Pestieau (2006, pp. 81–83).

[13] See, for example, the studies by Reinhardt (2000), Woodlander, Campbell, and Himmelstein (2003), Kotlikoff and Hagist (2005), and Cutler and Ly (2011).

bureaucratic because it does not need to spend so much on resources denying coverage to patients that might prove expensive for one reason or another. Universalist health coverage is also cheaper than means-tested coverage for the poor because it avoids having to investigate the legitimacy of poverty pleas. Similarly, tax-based public assistance to the poor is in turn cheaper than private charities' administrative expenses for raising donations.[14]

Similarly, on the tax side, broader taxes are also cheaper to administer. As countries develop and prosper, they tend to shift toward the broader kinds of taxes that economists consider more efficient. The typical shift was away from customs duties and other narrow taxes that might greatly disrupt choices (taxes on high-elasticity activities) toward broad taxes on all of a person's income or consumption. Across the first half of the twentieth century, the shift was toward broad income taxation; after that, the shift has been more toward VAT (value added taxation, a flat consumption tax) and sin taxes on addictive products causing external damages.

The same tax shift affected all prospering countries, whether they became welfare states or not. It is something that happened as government got bigger. Indeed, the tax shift helped them become bigger. Setting aside for the moment the incentive effects of this shift, we merely note here that a broad tax treating everybody similarly, and every source of income similarly, is easier and cheaper to administer. Figure 2 shows the dramatic decline in the administrative costs of collecting taxes in Britain since the eighteenth century and the United States since the nineteenth. Broader taxation reaps economies of scale to such a degree that today the Internal Revenue Service spends on administration only half a percent of the amount collected.[15] Welfare states have reaped similar economies as their budgets expanded on the basis of broader forms of taxation.

In addition, the tax mix used by welfare states looks more efficient even in conventional theory. Relative to the smaller-government rich economies, such as Canada, the United States, and Japan, the large-budget welfare states of Northern Europe get a greater share of their tax revenue from broad consumption taxes and sin taxes on harmful-addiction products such as tobacco, alcohol, and gasoline.[16] Canada, Japan, and the United States, by contrast, get a greater share of their tax revenue from direct taxes on income and wealth. Conventional economics favors broad sales taxation and sin taxes, and the sin taxes draw added support from those concerned with public health and environmental quality. While we lack reliable econometric evidence

---

[14] Lindert (2004, Ch. 3; and 2014).

[15] This omits, of course, the resource cost to taxpayers themselves of preparing their tax returns.

[16] See Kato (2003) and Lindert (2004, chapter 10).

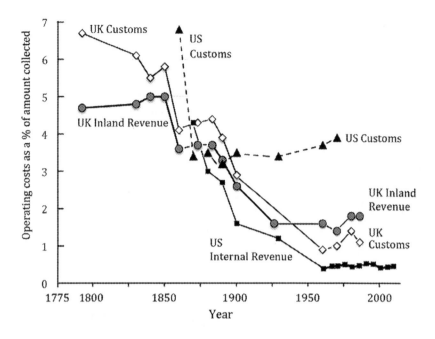

Figure 2 Tax collection costs as a percentage of the amounts collected by
central governments, USA and UK 1787/96–2011

The administrative cost share of tax collections are documented in Lindert,
Growing Public (2004, vol. 1, chapter 12), and updated in the IRS *Data Book*
(www.irs.gov/uac/Tax-Stats-2). I am indebted to Joel Slemrod for his directing
me to the updated IRS series.

that this kind of tax mix is really better for economic growth,[17] conventional
economists and economic conservatives *believe* that it is better. Ironically, then,
conventional theory favors the kinds of taxation used as a money machine for
large welfare states.

3.2 More Efficient Health Sectors

When it comes to public health care and health insurance, the superior efficiency of the more public approach is broadly recognized. Indeed, it is recognized by nearly all rich industrialized countries, even those whose overall
social budgets take less than 20 percent of GDP. For the health sectors, the
superiority of a dominant government role is almost as universally recognized,

---

[17] The closest thing to econometric support for this conventional hunch is the semi-robust result of
Kneller and co-authors (1999, and Gemmell et al. 2011) to the effect that indirect taxes are better
for growth than direct taxes.

as is the superiority of a heavily public approach to primary and secondary education.

The real contrast in health sectors is not between the high-spending welfare states and a host of free-market countries. Rather, it is a tragedy of American exceptionalism. With the United States as the dramatic exception, rich countries have achieved relative efficiency in the health sector, even though their institutions differ greatly. The following principles seem clear:

- Mandatory health insurance involves more efficient pooling of health risks than private voluntary insurance.
- In health care and pharmaceuticals, as in finance, the problems of market power and informational asymmetries require some variant on government price controls
- Taxpayers can cover over half of all health-sector expenditures. Even the United States has approached this outcome, albeit through a less efficient route.[18]

Note one other possible feature of a more public approach that is *not* necessary to health-sector efficiency: direct government *provision* of services. In health care, as in primary and secondary education, there has never been any clear demonstration that government should be the dominant direct supplier of the services, or the dominant employer. A country may achieve similarly decent results either through a (complex and messy) system of insuring private services in the presence of price controls, or through a (complex and messy) nationalized health service.

The low-performance outlier among rich OECD countries is, of course, the United States. Three international contrasts about health insurance and health care provide some circumstantial evidence favoring the performance of countries having more universal and publically funded health system. Two of these three facts are unknown to the American general public, while the third has received a great deal of media attention. The first fact, generally unappreciated, is one already cited above: America's mixed private–public health insurance has higher bureaucratic administrative costs than a universal government "single payer" scheme of health insurance (e.g. Canada, Germany) or a system dominated by nationalized provision of health services (e.g. England and Wales).[19] The second under-appreciated fact is about popular beliefs themselves. While people in all countries have complaints and fears

---

[18] The share of American health expenditures covered by taxpayers and government has risen from 37 percent in 1970 to 49 percent in 2014–2016 (stats.oecd.org).

[19] Again, see the studies by Reinhardt (2000), Woodlander et al. (2003), Kotlikoff and Hagist (2005), and Cutler and Ly (2011).

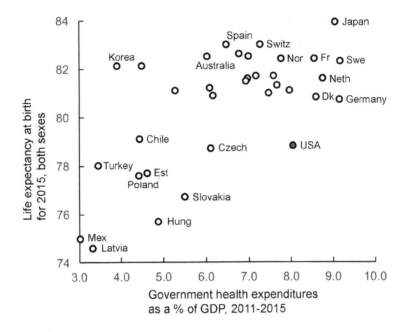

Figure 3a Life expectancy at birth versus public health spending, 34 OECD
countries

about their health care systems, Americans for decades have had a lower
opinion of their system than do people surveyed in other countries.

The third fact, given more media attention, is that the United States ranks
behind at least a dozen other countries in life expectancy. The pattern is not a
simple one relating to overall social spending. The world leader in life expectancy is Japan, a country with relatively modest social spending, though Japan's
social spending does tend to tilt toward public health. It could nonetheless be said
that people tend to live a bit longer in the average welfare state than in the United
States. The media have said so repeatedly, and have pointed out that a significant
part of the difference in life expectancy comes in the first year of life: American
babies do not survive as well as those in over a dozen other countries.

To underline America's perverse exceptionalism in health care, and to
suggest patterns and differences in the health care efforts of other countries,
Figures 3a and 3b summarize the complexity of health policy by simply noting
how countries' differences in life expectancy at birth, the most popular summary measure of healthiness, seems to relate to public fiscal effort and to
average national income. Figure 3a addresses a simple question: do countries
whose taxpayers cover more health care, as a share of their GDP, have better
life expectancy? The correlation is positive (0.64) and significant. Yet people

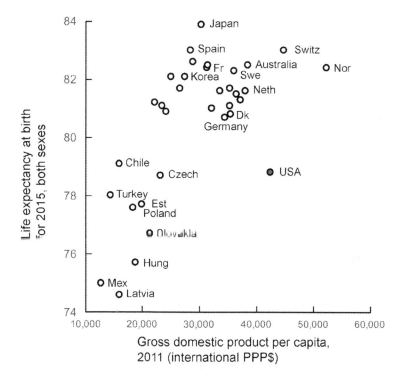

Figure 3b Life expectancy at birth versus GPD per capita, 34 OECD countries.
stats.oecd.org, via OECD iLibrary, accessed June 5, 2018.

are likely to live longer than 80 years either in countries that spend little on public health, as in Korea or Australia, or in welfare states with more expensive health budgets, such as France, Sweden, Denmark, or Germany. Among countries with high public health spending, the United States seems to get much less extra life. Figure 3b arrives at similar contrasts by relating life expectancy to average income levels (GDP per capita), a relationship some-times called the "Preston curve." Again, the overall correlation is positive (0.67), yet again the average American lives fewer years of life despite being richer than most countries.

How did the United States get into this position? Before reviewing the troubled history of American health care, we need to stress two cautionary points about the international contrasts in life expectancy. The first is that they do not just reflect the performance of the health care system. As best one can tell, the differences in survival are not due as much to differences in health care systems as to differences in life style. The slight shortening of life in America versus other rich countries is due primarily to sedentary lifestyle and diet. Second, the international contrasts are not between public and private systems, or between large-spending and small-spending countries. Rather they relate to a peculiarly vexed history of health insurance in the United States, a country that actually spends about as much publically, and spends much more privately, on health care than other rich countries.

At the center of America's health insurance problems is a pair of historical wrong turns that left the United States with too strong a reliance on voluntary employer-based health insurance. The first wrong turn came in World War II and the 1950s. Employer-based plans gained popularity in World War II, when wage controls prevented employers' competing for scarce workers by offering higher straight pay, but allowed them to offer attractive fringes. The new demand for employee health insurance was reinforced by the rise in unions' bargaining power. Then came a tax policy, enacted in 1943 and solidified in a 1954 Supreme Court ruling, that exempts employer contributions to employee health plans from taxation, either as corporate income or as employee income. Thus, one major reform left undone by the Congressional fight of 2010 is to remove the special subsidies on employer-based health coverage, and to push the industry toward offering plans that are more portable from job to job.[20]

A second costly wrong turn was taken in 1965, when the passage of Medicare confined public (alias "socialized") health insurance to those over 65 (plus the military). The second wrong turn was caused in part by the first. The passage of Medicare in 1965 was targeted at the elderly because they rightly feared facing costlier health care with no job to offer them coverage. Some have tried to reduce this elderly bias by extending Medicare to all age groups. In 2010, The Affordable Care Act succeeded in extending insurance toward the young, with extensions of Medicaid and the State Children's Health Insurance Program. It thus made partial steps toward making coverage more universal, while proceeding slowly enough to honor (to "grandfather") existing insurance arrangements. Yet one's 65th birthday still brings a jump in coverage, and this country's deficit in life expectancy among OECD countries is still worse before the age of 65 than after that birthday.[21] The health insurance trap, then, was specific to the United States, and not to all countries with smaller social budgets.

3.3 Better Development of Mothers' Human Capital

The welfare states also gain jobs and productivity through public policies that invest in career continuity and skills accumulation for mothers, indirectly also supporting their children's development. This matters a lot, now that such

---

[20] Starr (1982, pp. 310–344), Thomasson (2002, 2003).   [21] Eggleston and Fuchs (2012).

a large share of women's adulthood is career-oriented. Welfare states provide paid parental leaves and public day care with qualified providers. While the underlying rules are complex and hard to summarize, the policy differences among OECD countries are apparent in the fiscal efforts to promote work-life balance for parents, especially mothers, of newborns and infants.

Figure 4 contrasts the fiscal effort on behalf of "family benefits," the kind of (non-education) public spending devoted specifically to aiding families with minor children. The term "family benefits" could also be interpreted roughly as "mothers' benefits," given that mothers invest more time in childcare than do fathers. Figure 4 shows that, as of about 2012, welfare states such as Denmark, France, and Sweden spent more than 3 percent of GDP on supporting work-life balance for new mothers, whereas the United States, Japan, and others spent less than half this share. The contrasts are particularly strong for public funding of maternal leave around the time of childbirth. The United States is the only rich country that does not devote any taxpayer money at all to paid parental leave.[22]

Does the extra support for mothers pay off, when it is given? While it is not easy to estimate the productivity gains from such policies using micro-data, there is at least crude aggregate signs of strong gains. For the year 2006, Francine Blau's estimates for thirteen countries show that those countries with stronger support for families with children tend to have higher market wages for women relative to male wage rates. Figure 5 shows some of the differences in women's wage progress in seven of those thirteen countries over the period 1967–2006. These relative wage gains correlate positively with two of those three kinds of family support graphed for 2012 in Figure 4. The two kinds of support that correlate most suggestively with great gender wage equality are the cash transfers and the direct government provision of childcare services. The one kind of family support that correlates negatively with women's relative pay is the category "tax breaks for families," which portions out benefits that bear little relationship to women's careers.[23]

---

[22] For more detailed data, see the international data in the OECD Family Database, www.oecd.org /social/family/oecdfamilydatabase.htm#public_policy. For other summaries of differences in parental leave laws and public infant care, see Lindert (2004, vol. 1, 252–257 and 282–287). On the issue of having taxpayers cover parental leave, the text is here referring only to the absence of such US support at the federal level. Some states do provide subsidies and/or tax relief for maternal leave.

[23] While it is possible in principle that the higher female/male wage ratio in the countries with stronger family support might have reflected forces that lower male earnings, this seems very unlikely. Rather, the differences appear to be in policies that gave mothers the extra human capital that comes from not losing a career when a baby arrives. Indeed, other data show that the wage gap between males and females is specific to policy environments and to marital status: single women are very close to single men in their rates of pay, whereas married women, mostly mothers, are paid less in countries that support them less.

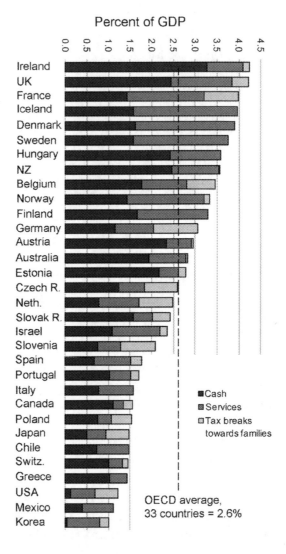

Figure 4 Government expenditures on family programs, 2012
Source = www.oecd.org/els/family/database.htm#public_policy/ PF1.1,
accessed June 7, 2018. The same source now covers these expenditure
categories for 1960–2013.

Public support accounted here only concerns public support that is exclusively
for families (e.g. child payments and allowances, parental leave benefits, and
childcare support). Spending recorded in other social policy areas, such as
health and housing, also assists families, but not exclusively, and is not
included here.

Data on tax breaks toward families are not available for Greece and Hungary.

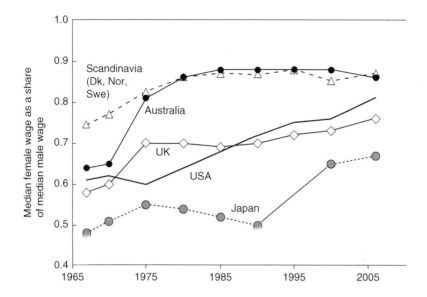

Figure 5 Female/male wage ratios in selected countries, 1967–2006

Note: For Denmark, Finland, Norway, and Sweden, figures for 1990 and before are for the manufacturing sector. For Germany, figures prior to 2000 are for West Germany. Data for Germany for 2000 and on are for the manufacturing sector.

A new series starts for France, Japan, and Switzerland in 2000.

The source is Blau (2012, p. 372), citing International Labour Organization, LABORSTA Internet database, http://laborsta.ilo.org.

The benefits of real-world government interventions on these welfare-state fronts, combined with the better tax mix of the high-budget welfare states, may help to explain why the statistical evidence has not turned up any negative effect of social transfers on GDP.

4 Real Demographic-Political Threat #1: Rising Immigration and Reaction against It

To see the real threats to the future of the welfare state, we need to look at two demographic changes and their relationships to politics.[24] This section turns to

---

[24] A third possible threat is set aside here because it is still just emerging and can, in principle, be handled with fine-tuning in institutional design. Participation in such non-standard employment types as self-employment, part-time employment, and independent contracting could erode access to social protection programs to insure earnings. Current and forthcoming writings by the OECD (2018, forthcoming) argue that erosion can be checked by (1) making social protection

the first demographic-and-political change, the likelihood of new restrictions on immigration in response to a rise in nativist backlash. Section 5 will confront population aging and the political "gray power" it may entail.

How would restrictions on immigration affect the generosity of social spending? The results would depend, of course, on the type of immigration being restricted – which skill groups would be cut, which age groups, and what emphasis on refugees versus economic migrants, for example. To mobilize the existing empirical literature, let us follow its tendency to summarize the effects of the observed recent mix of immigrants, without any detailed focus on a particular proposal for immigration restriction.[25]

The three main economic channels of influence of immigration on social spending would tend to run through

(1) its per-capita effects on government revenues, via its effects on GDP;
(2) the net fiscal surplus or deficit implied by existing support generosity for the foreign-born in different age groups; and
(3) its political effects on the generosity of social spending.

The estimated effects of restricting immigration through the first two channels are mirror images of the literature's estimated effects of recent immigration.

4.1 Immigrants' Effects on GDP and Government Revenue per Capita

The effects on government revenue, via effects on GDP, can conveniently draw on the literature estimating the effects of immigration on labor markets and productivity. That literature, while freely admitting the limitations of its evidence and its econometric estimation, generally concludes that the observed mix of immigration has probably raised GDP per capita a bit, especially in studies that try to guesstimate externalities.[26] The slight extra GDP in turns translates into a slight addition to government revenue, slightly improving the affordability of social programs. This bland and tentative positive result seems

---

access more uniform across employment types; (2) avoiding voluntary job-related insurance programs, which have proven vulnerable to adverse selection; and (3) making earnings insurance more portable by untying their links to specific employers.

[25] Even when scholars can take aim at the economic effects of a particular policy proposal, such as Brexit's likely restrictions on immigration, they have had to draw on estimates referring to the aggregate recent mix of immigrants, for want of specifics on which groups would be affected most severely. See Portes and Forte (2017, especially parts 3 and 4).

[26] For an overall survey, see Peri (2016). A pooled international test for twenty-two countries in recent years is offered by Boubtane et al. (2015). Recent positive summary appraisals of the GDP effects of immigration into the UK are Wadsworth et al. (2016) and Portes and Forte (2017).

to enjoy a consensus, despite the heated controversy over whether natives' wage rates are lowered, or raised, or unaffected.

4.2 Net Fiscal Effects Implied by Existing Entitlements

Even if immigrants contribute slightly to GDP and government revenue, such slight positives could be swamped by the extra demands that immigrants place on social expenditure programs. There is widespread fear that immigrants are a net fiscal burden, for which the already-arrived native population must pay. Opinion surveys have shown that fears of immigrants' negative fiscal effects loom even larger than fears of such effects on labor market effect as their taking jobs away or lowering wages.[27]

Such a fiscal burden often exists. The net fiscal effects of extra immigrants depend on one's time horizon, however. Table 2 summarizes this dependence conceptually, drawing on plausible longer-run simulations like those run by Ronald D. Lee and Timothy Miller (2000), by the OECD (2013), and by the UK's Migration Advisory Committee (2018, chapter 4).

Suppose we take the usual short-run view, in the top row of Table 2, asking "Do today's extra immigrants cause a net drain on government budgets in this same year?"[28] They often do so, since extra immigrants' families typically are a net drain through the host country's child-related social programs such as education. If this drain is greater than the tax revenues collected from adult immigrants, helping to pay for pensions and other public programs, then immigrants do indeed cause a net fiscal drain this year. Fiscal-demographic simulations suggest that the net short-run fiscal effect is indeed negative. A typical mix of immigrant age groups is so tilted toward the young that the costs of child-centered social programs yield a negative net result for the first 12–15 years after an immigrant arrival. This short-run negative effect would also show up in immigrants' use of non-contributory aid to those of working age. As OECD

---

[27] See the survey evidence in Dustmann and Preston (2007), using English whites' responses for 1983–1990; and Boeri (2010, pp. 662–668), using the European Social Survey of 2002. Curiously, both studies find that the Nordic countries, where immigrants are a relative fiscal burden, believe more that the fiscal contributions of immigrants are positive on balance, whereas countries like Austria, Britain, and Spain believe more in a fiscal drain that does not seem to exist in their cases. Differences in perceptions seem to drive differences in social policy, rather than vice versa. For 2018 survey evidence on perceptions about immigrants' fiscal effects in six countries, see Alesina, Miano, and Stantcheva 2018.

[28] Most quantifications of the fiscal effects of immigration concentrate on this short-run, or pay-as-you-go, effect (e.g. Boeri 2010, pp. 656–661; OECD 2013, pp. 144–160). A strength of the Lee-Miller simulation is that it traces out the longer-run effects that follow from demographic likelihoods. On the other hand, their simulation omits behavioral effects, market-equilibrium effects, and the impacts of different mixes of immigrants. For theoretical and empirical warnings on these other fronts, see Preston (2014).

Table 2 The fiscal effects of extra immigrants depend on the question you ask about them

The question you ask	Effects through Public pensions	Effects through public schooling, aid to young
The "pay as you go" question: Are today's immigrants a net burden on native taxpayers, right now, "pay-as-you-go"?	**No**, immigrants pay for natives' public pensions.	**Yes**, immigrant children subsidized by native taxpayers.
The "one lifetime" question: Is one wave of immigrants a net burden on native taxpayers over the life span of the immigrants and their descendants?	**Yes**, if immigrants have lower lifetime earnings, they get an above-average rate of return on pensions, at expense of other taxpayers.	**No**, immigrants' children repay the rest of society in productivity and taxes.
The "many generations" question: Are today's immigrants, plus their children and grandchildren to 2100, a net fiscal burden?	**No**, they become heavy net taxpayers, like others.	**No**, they become heavy net taxpayers, like others.

Notes: If one could pay for pensions and other social transfers out of government debt, and out of the reserves of the pension system, then the left-hand side of the equation should be modified to include payments of taxes in earlier and later years, not just the current year. Yet they have to be paid sooner or later, and the problem remains essentially as stated in this pure same-year version of PAYGO.

Note another simplification here: This section ignores non-transfer spending, such as national defense, highway construction, and basic government payrolls. Taxation here refers only to those taxes that are spent on pensions and other social transfers.

economists have rightly emphasized, the short-run fiscal impact depends above all on the host country's success or failure in helping the foreign-born find jobs.[29]

---

[29] For a meta-analysis of net fiscal impact research on immigrants in the OECD countries, see (OECD 2013, chapter 3 and appendices). Most of the analysis tends to address the first question, the short-run, pay-as-you-go question, of our Table 2.

Next, suppose one takes a somewhat longer view, asking Table 2's second question about the net fiscal effects over the whole lifetimes of the first generation of new immigrants. Now the net effect is probably positive. True, the immigrants in old age probably get a net transfer from others, because public pension systems are typically designed to be progressive, giving a high rate of return to lower-income earners, such as first-generation immigrants. Yet while that first generation is aging, its children have already become productive adults, paying positive taxes instead of needing school money. These tax contributions should outweigh any intra-cohort redistributions toward foreign-born pensioners.

Finally, when we consider the whole lifetimes of not only the extra immigrants but also their children and grandchildren, the net fiscal effects become clearly positive, as again suggested in Table 2. We know that the eventual fiscal results are clearly positive because in the long run the immigrants and their descendants pay more in taxes than they get in targeted transfers, just like the rest of society. So the long-run fiscal effect of extra immigration is clearly positive.[30]

There remains the third channel of economic impacts, running through the possible political effects on the generosity of social spending. The positive fiscal effects of immigrants and their descendants may be politically trumped by negative perceptions, especially in the wake of a large influx of refugees. Prevailing opinions can still be negative about the same fiscal effects, and about the negative effects on some native workers' earning power, not to mention cultural phobias and fears of terrorism. Alberto Alesina and co-authors find that natives of six countries greatly overestimate not only the amount of immigration, but also the net fiscal burden imposed by the average immigrant.[31] That kind of reaction has gained increasing political force in Europe and the United States, where the new nativism rides the wave of anti-immigrant sentiment. There is a fair chance that coalitions of such nativist parties and more established conservative parties could take power in several countries.

---

[30] Estimates based on data from several countries around the turn of the century yield net fiscal benefits from migrants that tend to be near zero over the short run, with more positive net results than negative ones. See OECD (2013, chapter 3) for the assumptions and time horizons used. Note that the simulations run by Lee and Miller (2000) do not refer to a large refugee influx, since their parameters were drawn from calm time periods.

[31] Alesina et al. (2018, esp. pp. 28ff). The survey was taken in early 2018 in Germany, France, Italy, Sweden, the UK, and the USA. The sample sizes were 4,500 for the USA, 4,001 for the UK, 4,001 for Germany, 4,000 for France, 4,000 for Italy, and 2,004 for Sweden, for a total of 22,506 respondents.

4.3 Political Effects of Immigration on the Generosity of Social Spending

Will a rise in anti-immigrant sentiment undermine the fiscal generosity of the welfare states? There is reason to think so. The 2018 surveys conducted by Alesina and co-authors find that generous redistribution is indeed undermined by that perception of immigrants' being heavy beneficiaries of redistribution.[32] While the threat seems real, the mechanism is not so obvious. The outcome will surely depend on the form that the backlash takes.

Let us consider three kinds of cases in which there would *not* be much threat to social spending on natives. First consider the possibility that immigration is simply blocked. In such a case, immigrants would cease to be a short-run budgetary burden, aside from the cost of enforcing the barriers at the border. In such a case, social spending on the native population can continue as before.[33]

A second, and nearly equivalent, possibility is that the government reacts to the anti-immigrant spirit with a combination of blocking boat people and over-border refugees, while continuing to admit the highly skilled. Such a combination is being practiced by such non-welfare-states as Australia and Switzerland. Here again, there is little threat to social programs for established citizens, since the skilled immigrants passing through the filter will quickly become net taxpayers.

A third possibility is that immigrants are still allowed to enter, but the government discriminates against them in its provision of social services. Practicing such discrimination, also known as "welfare chauvinism," would make it easier to avoid dilution of benefits for natives. To what extent have immigrant-receiving countries practiced such discrimination? The real test will be the policy reactions to Europe's heavy refugee inflow of 2014–2015. That test is currently in progress. Thus far, in any case, countries accepting immigrants have been unwilling to saddle themselves with immigrants who are not entitled to basic social services.[34]

---

[32] Ibid. While they find that support for redistribution is undermined by the belief that it disproportionately benefits immigrants, such support is not much affected by the perceived size of the immigration inflow.

[33] This conjecture sets aside the possible slightly positive effects of immigrants on GDP and government revenue per capita, the kinds of effects discussed by Peri (2016).

[34] A near approach to cultural chauvinism, receiving immigrants while denying them basic services, threatened to arise when Californians passed Proposition 187 in 1994. The proposition called for denying public K-12 education and other public services to the families of those non-US citizens who had entered the state without legal documentation. However, Proposition 187 was struck down by the state's Supreme Court, and has never been implemented.

The countries most likely to translate heavy immigration, plus strong opposition to that immigration, into a reduction of universal social entitlements would be those welfare-state countries that absorb large numbers of refugees, without skill requirements, yet remain unwilling to discriminate against them in the provision of basic social services. The highest likelihood of such a dilution of universal welfare state benefits seems to face Sweden and Germany since the mass influx of Syrian, Iraqi, Afghan, and other refugees in this decade, especially since 2014. In these two prime-target countries, a visible strain on social entitlement standards may soon appear. The strain will be especially great if the recent arrivals and their families continue to have a lower employment rate than natives.[35]

5 Real Demographic-Political Threat #2. Aging and Gray Power

5.1 The Curse of Longer Life: Something Has To Give

Something has to give in pension policy in the twenty-first century, as many have long warned. Those over the age of 65 will go on rising as a share of the adult population, just as they have done for more than a century. The ratios of the elderly to those of working age are rising most ominously in East Asia and Italy, but no country is exempt. Since the 1970s, the main cause has been the upward march of senior life expectancy. The life expectancy of seniors is shooting up rapidly, presenting all pension calculations with a possible curse of unexpectedly long life.[36] The natural solution of having people work to later ages, in order to hold fixed the share of their adult lives spent at work, was undermined by a decline in the average age of male retirement in the late twentieth century, though this has historically contributed less to the lengthening of retirement than has the improvement in life expectancy.[37]

The balance between younger people paying into pensions for the elderly and elderly people drawing pension benefits is thus shifting. So we are warned

---

[35] The issue has already achieved prominence in Sweden. On the one hand, Sweden's conservatives deny that cutting the welfare state is their object, knowing that the welfare state remains popular. In February 2011 the leader of Sweden's Right-Wing "Sweden Democrats" Party, not to be confused with the Social Democratic Party that has governed Sweden most of the time since 1932, was explicit about this: "We believe in the welfare state," while also voicing suspicions about Sweden's mosques and Islamic community groups. The threat is real, though no reduction of universal benefits has yet occurred.

[36] On the recent acceleration of senior survival rates, see Eggleston and Fuchs (2012).

[37] For historical retirement trends from the United States see, for example, Costa (1998). One should note that the trend toward earlier male retirement has reversed itself in many OECD countries since 2000.

repeatedly by the media. This demographic fact of life has a clear implication for the two largest, and now fastest rising, kinds of social spending. Both public health expenditures and public pensions are paid more generously to the elderly than to the younger population.[38] Quantitative projections of future government expenditures on public health in OECD countries suggest that population aging would raise their share of GDP noticeably by mid-century, even though this aging effect has accounted for less than half the observed rise in public health expenditures over the last few decades.[39]

To identify the clearest threat to public budgets from population aging, let us focus on the stark choices facing public pensions alone, even though the inter-generational options would have looked the same if we had included public health expenditures by age group.

As each nation's population gets older, social-budget pressures mount. To summarize the choices that have to be made, we need to look at a crude but insightful steady-state accounting equation. For long-run equilibrium, the government social-transfer budget must show a balance between the taxes or contributions paid into the social programs and the benefits paid out, both to the elderly and to others. That is,

$$\text{Net tax revenues devoted to social transfers} = \text{Pension benefits}^{40} + \text{non-pension social transfers}$$

To show how population aging puts pressure on this social budget equation, let us use a few definitions:

B = benefits per elderly person
N_{young} = number of working-age adults
N_{old} = population of retirees (over 65, say)
r = share of the working-age population receiving non-pension benefits (public health care, family aid, unemployment compensation, etc.)
t = share of income paid in taxes (minus non-transfer government spending)
u = non-pension social benefits per recipient of working age
Y = national income per person.

---

[38] For the age patterns of public health and long-term care benefits as a share of GDP in nineteen European countries and Australia, see de la Maisonneuve and Oliveira Martins (2013). The same patterns are documented for Japan in Nozaki, Kashiwase, and Saito (2014), and for the United States in US Centers for Medicare and Medicaid Services (2012).

[39] See, for example Nozaki et al. (2014).

[40] In what follows, I use the term "pensions" as a convenient synonym for benefit payments received by the elderly. In terms of official OECD data on social expenditures, payments to the elderly include not just what the governments and the OECD call "pensions," but two broader categories: "elderly benefits" (they include pensions as a component) plus "survivor benefits." I would also have added medical benefits accruing to the elderly had the data permitted.

To have a balanced system, with no surplus or deficit, then the net tax revenues taken from workers each year for this purpose must just equal the benefits paid to both kinds of recipients. So each year, out of $GDP = Y_{young} * N_{young}$, the government collects taxes and distributes them to the elderly and to younger recipients of transfers:

$$t * Y_{young} * N_{young} = (B * N_{old}) + (u * r * N_{young}).$$

This basic equation for the social-transfer budget can be re-arranged to show that

$$(N_{old}/ N_{young}) = (t * Y_{young} - u * r)/B$$

The left-hand side is sure to rise, as every national population in the world eventually gets older. How can the right-hand side rise to preserve the equality? Of course, a healthy rise in productivity growth, a rise in (Y_{young}), could lift all boats. Yet if societies cannot simply will faster growth, there remain *these unattractive choices:*

(1) **Tax hikes**: The nation can raise the tax rate on current workers' earnings and property (t).
(2) **Restraining support for the young**. The nation can cut non-pension transfers per young person (u * r), either by lowering the benefit payments for entitled recipients (u), or by cutting the share of young persons who are entitled to any benefit (r); or it can just "restrain" them by not letting them grow as fast as productivity (Y_{young}).
(3) **Direct restraint on elderly support**: The nation can cut pensions per elderly person (B), either by postponing benefits to older retirement ages or by slashing pension rates across the board. Or it can just restrain them, again, by not letting them grow as fast as average productivity (Y_{young}).

None of these options is popular, but at least one of them has to happen. To avoid the long-run unsustainability of raising tax rates indefinitely, and to avoid investing less in the future health and productivity of the young, countries would have to choose among the options for direct restraints on elderly support – i.e.

(3a) incentivizing the elderly to keep working longer; or
(3b) keeping annual benefits per retiree from rising as fast as productivity.

In other words, to avoid raising taxes forever and to avoid cutting the support for the young relative to average incomes, this restraint must follow:

As the share of elderly rises, their annual transfer benefits past the age of 65
cannot forever continue rising as fast as the average annual incomes of those
of working age[41]

This clear warning is both softer and louder than it may sound at first. Softer, in the sense that it does not mean pensions have to drop in real purchasing power. Pensions could still keep up ahead of the cost of living – it's just that they cannot grow as fast as earned incomes per person of working age, which historically grow at about 1.8 percent a year, adjusting for inflation.

Yet the warning should sound louder when one realizes that it applies to the future of *any* kind of provision for old age, no matter how private or public. The curse of longer life is not specific to Social Security or other public pensions. It is the same even if you rely only on your own savings for old age. To plan ahead, if you live to age 65, you are likely to live to 85 even at today's survival rates. Your grandfather only had to plan on living about 14 years more, if he were to reach age 65. Even in such an individualist calculation, your annual consumption after your 65th birthday has to be a lower share of annual earnings than in the past, because you'll live more years. So it's not a problem of government pensions, but a problem facing *any* pension plans, be they individual savings, private job-based pensions, or public pensions.

Thus, as long as pension support per elderly person keeps in step with wage and salary rates, population aging threatens to raise the share of GDP devoted to subsidizing the elderly. To avoid paying for this with an upward march in tax rates, or with cutbacks in public spending on more productivity investments in the young, society needs to trim the relative generosity of annual pension subsidies. That, however, is not the current direction of movement in most industrialized, and aging, countries.

How have different countries responded to their population aging since 1980? Table 3 compares snapshots taken of ten countries' social transfers toward the elderly and toward those under 65 in the two years 1980 and 2013, while Figure 6 follows annual pension support ratios for six of these countries. The ten countries consist of a first-listed five that have restrained their public support for the elderly enough to buy time, and a second-listed five countries that have failed to keep the elderly-support budget from rising ominously as a share of GDP. To follow this division of results, let us initially focus on the first two columns in Table 3. The age share in the first column, corresponding to (N_{old} / N_{young}) in the equations above, times the second

---

[41] Note again that the division here is not between those working and those retired, but rather between those of working age and the elderly. For this reason, changes in retirement rates for different age groups do affect the apparent rates of transfers paid or received.

Table 3 Elderly age shares and social transfers, 10 OECD countries, 1980–2013

	Elderly pop (65–up) as % of 18–64	Support ratio for elderly (%)	Rel. support for non-elderly as % of elder sup.	Pub health & incap. exp. as % of GDP.	All social transfers as % of GDP
In 1980 –					
Australia	16.1	22.8	14.8	4.6	10.3
Germany	25.8	40.8	11.7	8.3	21.8
Sweden	27.2	28.8	30.5	5.1	24.8
UK	25.3	22.5	34.9	5.4	15.8
USA	18.8	32.3	11.0	4.6	12.8
France	23.5	39.8	19.7	8.1	20.2
Greece	22.1	23.5	4.1	4.1	9.9
Italy	22.2	38.5	7.0	7.2	17.4
Spain	19.1	31.9	14.0	6.3	15.0
Japan	14.3	27.9	18.2	1.6	10.2
In 2013 –					
Australia	23.5	22.3	31.7	9.0	18.7
Germany	33.3	30.4	24.2	10.0	24.8
Sweden	31.9	31.2	35.1	4.6	27.4
UK	27.9	23.9	42.3	9.2	22.1
USA	22.3	31.2	12.2	9.4	18.8
France	30.4	46.9	24.6	10.3	31.5
Greece	31.7	55.2	9.5	7.2	28.0
Italy	35.0	46.8	12.9	8.5	28.6
Spain	28.1	42.6	19.7	8.9	26.3
Japan	42.3	28.6	28.8	2.4	23.1
Absolute percentage-point difference, 1980–2013 –					
Australia	7	–0.5	17	4	8
Germany	7	–10	12	2	3
Sweden	5	2	5	–0.4	3
UK	3	1	7	4	6
USA	4	–1	1	5	6

Table 3 (cont.)

	Elderly pop (65–up) as % of 18–64	Support ratio for elderly (%)	Rel. support for non-elderly as % of elder sup.	Pub health & incap. exp. as % of GDP.	All social transfers as % of GDP
France	7	7	5	2	11
Greece	10	32	5	3	18
Italy	13	8	6	1	11
Spain	9	11	6	3	11
Japan	28	1	11	1	13

Sources for populations by age group: www.census.gov/population/international, and United Nations online.

Source for all public expenditures = OECD iLibrary/statistics.

Source for GDP in current prices = http://gpih.ucdavis.edu/GDP.htm.

Elderly share of adult population = (population ages 65–up) / (population ages 18–64), both sexes combined.

Support ratio for the elderly = (public expenditures on elderly and survivor benefits, per person 65 and up) / (GDP per person 18–64).

Relative support for the non-elderly, versus support for the elderly = (all public social transfers other than elderly benefits, survivor benefits, health, and incapacity benefits) / (pension support ratio for the elderly, as defined above).

Pub health & incap. exp. = all government expenditures on public health and incapacity benefits.

All social transfers = public social expenditures as defined by the OECD, i.e. excluding public expenditures on education.

For France, the starting year is 1985, not 1980.

For Greece, the ending year is 2012, not 2013.

column's elderly-support ratio, corresponding to B, should equal the share of transfers in GDP. The danger, again, is that this product should rise.

As can be seen in both Table 3 and Figure 6, the first five countries have been preventing pensions from rising much as a share of GDP. The most visibly successful of the five is Germany, where pensions have lost 10 percent of their original 1980 ratio to GDP per person of working age.[42] Figure 6 traces the

---

[42] Similar restraint, with pensions falling behind average income growth, was also achieved by New Zealand (with a 20 percent drop in the elderly support ratio easily exceeding the rise of 6 percent in the elderly population share), the Netherlands (with an 11 percent drop in the support ratio exceeding a 9 percent rise in the elderly share), and to a lesser extent Ireland (with no population aging at all and a modest 2.5 percent drop in the elderly support ratio as defined

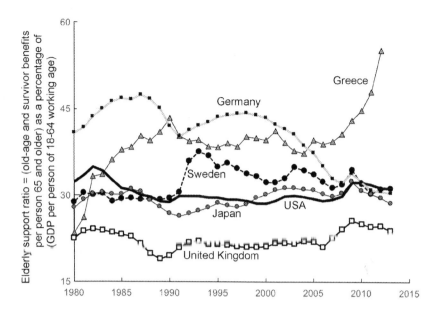

Figure 6 Elderly-support ratios in six OECD countries, 1980–2013
See sources and notes to Table 3 below.

timing of this restraint, showing that it has spanned a quarter of a century since about 1987, and was not concentrated on the moment of Germany's national reunification. The overall net decline made it possible for Germany to avoid any sizeable increase in either pensions or all social transfers as shares of GDP over these 33 years. The other four of the first five countries also responded to the aging problem, albeit less resolutely. Australia, Sweden, the United Kingdom, and the United States, which were faced with only slow aging, maintained stable elderly-support ratios over this third of a century, enabling themselves to raise social budgets by only a small share of GDP, as shown in the final column.

By contrast, the five other countries in Table 3 failed to offset, and actually reinforced, the budget expansion accompanying their more rapid aging. Of these, the most extreme case has been Greece, of course. For Greece, the problem has indeed centered on the public sector, which spent unwisely on pensions and the Athens Olympics. With unsustainable public pensions and crashing GDP, Greece's support ratio soared after 2007, as Figure 6 dramatizes.

here) and Canada (very little aging, partly offset by a 2 percent reduction in the elderly-support ratio). The responses of Belgium, Denmark, and Switzerland resembled those of Australia, Sweden, the United Kingdom, and the United States in leaving the pension support ratio largely unchanged in the face of slight population aging.

The other three Mediterranean countries (France, Italy, and Spain) also shifted toward offering more public support per elderly person, relative to GDP per capita, even as their populations aged.[43] Japan, the final country shown here, managed to keep its pension support ratio from rising. Yet in the face of having a 28 percent rise in the number of elderly per person of working age, keeping the elderly-support ratio steady leads to as much budgetary stress as experienced by the four Mediterranean countries shown in Table 3. Probably as a result, Japan and the four Mediterranean countries ended up raising their overall social transfer budgets about twice as much as the five countries showing more pension restraint.

5.2 Elderly Bias in Certain Countries since the 1960s

The further expansion of government social budgets has changed focus over the last half-century, drifting away from those human investments having the greatest GDP gains and toward support for the elderly and the middle classes.[44] Curiously, the shift has occurred mainly in countries that are not welfare states. This section charts the mission shift, first viewing where it occurred, then examining its fingerprints in terms of social expenditure behavior, and finally conjecturing about its efficiency consequences and implications for the future.

Since the 1960s, poverty rates have been reduced much more successfully for the elderly than for children or persons of working age. So say the averages over groups of OECD countries.[45] In large groupings of OECD countries, we see a clear divide around age 50. All age groups up to 50 years of age experienced an increased poverty share relative to the population as a whole, while those above 50 shifted out of poverty faster than the whole population. In the United States, for example, poverty declined dramatically for those over 65 but not for children between 1959 and 2010. Over this half-century, the poverty share fell from about 34 percent of the elderly population to 9 percent, whereas it fell only from 28 percent to 22 percent among children.[46]

The drift toward lowering poverty rates more for the elderly than for children and those in working age is clearly tied to a bias in expenditure policy, particularly in certain countries. To show this, one needs to avoid just examining

---

[43] Similar ominous rises in the elderly-support ratio have occurred since 1980 in Finland, Israel, and Portugal, and slightly so for Denmark.

[44] For an in-depth history of the politics of the postwar drift toward the elderly and toward less progressive social spending, see Baldwin (1990).

[45] OECD, (2008, chapter 5, figure 5.5), updated September 12, 2008. In all that follows, the concept of transfers toward the elderly, or "pension subsidies," should be thought of as being measured by only the non-contributory part of elderly benefits.

[46] See www.census.gov/hhes/www/poverty/data/historical/people.html, as accessed December 31, 2011.

social expenditures as shares of GDP, which can be driven by the age group shares of total population. Table 3 provides some hints in its center column, which measures the government transfers to the non-elderly, per person in the age group, relative to the per-person transfers to the elderly. This measure of relative age-group policy takes on particularly low values, both in 1980 and in 2013, for Germany, the United States, Greece, and Italy. This is an initial clue that some countries are, more than other countries, sacrificing investments in the young in order to prop up the disposable incomes of the elderly.

A more telling kind of expenditure measure, available for a greater number of countries, is the percentage by which poverty for each age group has been reduced by net transfers from government. Figure 7 contrasts the international patterns in such net transfers by age group.[47] As far as aiding the elderly poor is concerned, OECD countries have generally done their job, cutting the poverty shares of their elderly populations by better than half in almost all countries, as shown in Panel A of Figure 7. So say the OECD estimates for most countries in both 1995 and 2005, which can be viewed as increases across the late twentieth century, since government transfer budgets were too small to reduce poverty very much as of the 1950s.

Countries differed far more in their willingness to cut poverty among younger groups, both in 1995 and again in 2005, according to the remaining panels of Figure 7. Unlike the similarity of all OECD countries in their pension subsidies (Figure 7A), the age pattern reveals the wide gap in poverty reduction for those of working age (Figure 7B) and for children (Figure 7 C). By the turn of the century, the poverty-cutting results were dramatically lower for Japan, the United States, and other non-welfare-states than for the Nordics and the Czech Republic. Particularly striking is that Italy, whose large share of social spending in GDP would qualify for welfare-state status under the 20-percent rule, has directed so little of its social budgets toward cutting poverty. Again, as elsewhere in the Mediterranean (and in South America's Southern Cone), social transfers go to the elderly, largely those with privileged occupations in their earlier careers.

Has favoring the support of the elderly, and investing less in those under the age of 65, been something costly in terms of GDP? The answer depends on the social-budget counterfactual one chooses to pose. Here are the two leading candidates:

---

[47] The source of these insightful estimates, (OECD 2008), unfortunately excludes Austria, Greece, Hungary, Iceland, Korea, Poland, Spain, and any Latin American countries.

For alternative measures of the elderly bias in social expenditures, 1985–2000, see Lynch (2001, 2006). Her measures compare support ratios in the form of (social expenditure benefits / person in the age range) for the elderly versus those of working age.

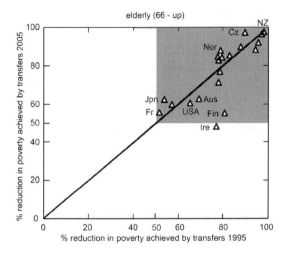

A. For the elderly (ages 66 and up)

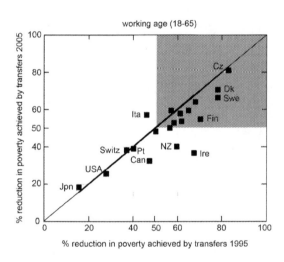

B. For those of working age (18–65 years)

Counterfactual A: Take some of the government money spent on the elderly, and
shift it toward the leading kinds of social programs for children and those of
working age (education, preventive out-patient health care for children, worker
retraining, etc.).

Counterfactual B: Privatize pensions, by reducing taxes and mandating individual savings accounts for old age.

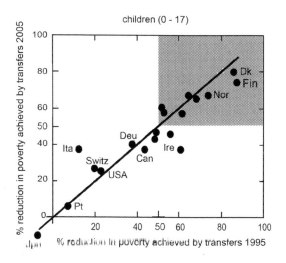

C. For children (0–17 years)

Figure 7 Poverty reduction achieved through fiscal Net transfers, 1995 and 2005
OECD (2008, figure 5.12 and its link to a data spreadsheet).

Thus far, the text has implied that we are comparing actual practice with Counterfactual A, and for this comparison the answer is clearly yes, the bias in favor of the elderly is clearly costly in terms of GDP. That is evident from the simple fact that investing in human development brings a higher return, the earlier the stage of cognitive and career development. The importance of this point has recently been underlined in the writings of Pedro Carneiro and James Heckman, among others, finding that even among children, the rate of return seems higher, the earlier the child age at which parents and society intervene.[48]

By contrast, comparison of actual practice with Counterfactual B suggests no clear difference in GDP. For all we can tell from twentieth-century data, individual saving and tax-financed saving can yield the same GDP result with appropriate adjustments of parameters in programs targeting the elderly. One might note that universal public pension programs, such as Social Security in the United States, are administered with lower bureaucratic costs and lower default risk than private pension plans or individual investments. On the other hand, there is ample reason to fear that the political process would underfund public pensions. Twentieth-century panel data have not allowed us to deny that

[48] Carneiro and Heckman (2003), Hoynes and Schanzenbach (2018), and the sources cited there.

there is a zero net effect on GDP from choosing public pensions over mandated private individual pensions. Thus the historic drift toward funneling tax money to the elderly either has cost GDP or not, depending on whether one wants to consider Counterfactual A or Counterfactual B.

5.3 What Role for Gray Power?

If there is no clear gain in GDP from shifting social insurance and assistance toward the elderly, why have so many societies been drifting toward it? One possible answer might be gray power. We know that the elderly tend to have greater than average turnout as voters in democratic elections.[49] Has the recent aging of populations reinforced the political power of the elderly plus those approaching old age?

The idea of rising gray power would gain initial credibility if population aging were accompanied by redistributive outcomes in favor of the elderly. Over the sweep of the last two centuries, the generosity of annual support for each elderly person definitely advanced in step with the aging of the adult population, as one would expect if gray power were on the rise. While more recent international experience offers some support, it only offers weak support to this initial premise of the gray power hypothesis. For the cross-section of ten countries in Table 3, it is only slightly true that countries with more aged populations have higher levels of, or faster growth in, their elderly-support ratios and in overall social spending. The departures from any average curve relating aging to pension generosity seem as wide, and as deserving of a deeper explanation, as the slope of the curve itself. Why, for example, does Spain offer an elderly-support ratio of 42 percent versus only 24 percent in the United Kingdom in 2013, when Spain's elderly-population share had only just caught up to Britain's? A more satisfactory explanation of the recent history illustrated in Table 3 will have to wait on a more detailed comparative political history.

5.4 Formulas That Have Worked for Public Pensions

Whatever the underlying causal explanation of the differential rise of support for the elderly, economists have identified broad policy formulas that can adjust our pensions to longer life spans. Here are three formulas that would make the non-contributory part of public pensions sustainable indefinitely, formulas that private savings plans should also try to emulate.

---

[49] See, for example, the voting rates by age groups in recent decades, as documented internationally by Wolfinger and Rosenstone (1980), Solijonov (2016, pp. 38–41), AARP (2017), Burn-Murdoch (2017), and United States Elections Project (ongoing).

The first formula is one on which a few countries have already done their homework quite well, and just need to follow through. The formula is this:

Keep the share of adult life spent on non-contributory public pensions from rising, by extending the working age for each benefit rate in proportion to adult life expectancy.

Germany has taken steps down this retirement-delaying path since 1992. So has the United States, thanks to the 1983 Greenspan Commission on Social Security Reform. America has advanced the age of "full" retirement benefits from 65 to 67 for those born after 1960. The gradual formula adopted in 1983 wisely follows the strategy of "grandfathering," by not hitting those of middle age with a shock to their life plans.

Yet the news about accelerating senior longevity means that pension programs must continue to be adjusted. Seniors are increasingly healthy, and the share of them in poverty has declined, so it is not unreasonable for them to receive full pension benefits only if they work the same share of their adult lives as did their parents. Fixing the share of adult life at work would mean something like this, using the American case as an illustration: To receive the year 2007's retirement benefit as a percentage of average earnings at any given age, one must work 51.6 percent of one's life expectancy for males, and 41.5 percent for females, as was done in 2007. Longer careers could keep pace with longer adult life expectancy.

The second formula builds in an automatic adjustment of the work-retirement balance to the longevity trend. Borrowing from the "notional defined contribution" pension reform that Sweden set up in the 1990s, the formula is this:

Index the retirement benefits for each cohort to life expectancy at age 60.

That is, while every individual's annual pension benefits are still tied to his or her lifetime earnings history, they are indexed to the senior survival odds of everybody in his or her birth cohort. Thus if you were born in 1980, and you worked from 2000 to 2045, your annual pension benefits would be tied to your earnings over those years, divided by an index that is tied to the age-60 life expectancy calculated from survival outcomes around the year 2040. The longer your cohort of people is expected to live, the less your benefits each year, though of course your benefits are likely to continue for more years. This helps maintain aggregate balance in the pension budget.

The third formula is also patterned after Swedish practice since the 1990s:

Index annual pension payouts to recent GDP per working-age person.[50]

Pensioners' benefits from Social Security should share in the fortunes of the economy. When there is a boom, pensioners share in it, by automatic formula. By the same formula, pensioners share the pain of a recession as much as others. In an unlikely Great Depression extreme, their ultimate safety net would be the same as for the young: public support for the poor plus medical care.

Pre-commitment to such pre-determined formulae could remove the pension parameters from the political arena. Of course, social contracts can only make political pre-commitment easier. They cannot guarantee it. Even Sweden softened its pre-set formula very slightly in response to the 2008–2009 slump. Under the original formula, the government was obligated to cut benefits for the two years 2010–2011. Afraid to follow through on the cuts in 2010, an election year for Parliament, officials changed the formula to stretch the reductions out over more years. Yet the system remains intact, and it still works.

Nonetheless, in pensions as in human investments in health and mothers' careers, welfare state Sweden stands out as a leader in rational solutions to social concerns.

6 Conclusion

The imagined economic threats to the welfare state have not materialized. No welfare state has become poor. Nor has there been any international "race to the bottom" in taxes and social spending. Productive people and their wealth did not flee from the welfare states any faster than other productive people and their wealth arrived. The welfare state looks like a Darwinian survivor in the global economy.

As we have seen, this favorable economic outcome did not just emerge from a statistical black box. There are plausible reasons for expecting such an outcome, and real-world governments have appreciated that broad safety nets and investing taxpayers' money in human development will raise human productivity. They have financed the universal social programs with broad taxes, at low administrative cost, using a mix of taxes that conventional economics would have preferred.

---

[50] I have oversimplified Sweden's system of pensions and elderly care, which is well described in Knuse (2010) and Edebalk (2010). Instead of an index tied to GDP per working-age adult, Sweden uses two other index factors that yield a similar result. The economic aggregate is wages and salaries per employed person, not GDP per person 18–64. And Sweden backs up its pension stability with an additional trigger that goes off whenever the pension fund's "Balance ratio" BR = capitalized assets / capitalized obligations drops below 1.

In the process, the large-budget welfare states are world leaders in achieving an egalitarian society with lower income inequality and lower poverty, while maintaining relatively steady trust and social peace. Perhaps one key to this peaceful egalitarian achievement is the fact that their progressivity was achieved not through friction-causing steeply progressive taxes but through universalism in their social expenditures. The lower- and middle-income classes that most favored social insurance in fact paid for much of it themselves.

The real threats to the welfare state are not economic, but rather arise as political responses to demographic movements. One real threat is that political backlash against a rising influx of refugees could bring a retreat from universalist welfare programs. This threat is probably confined to countries like Sweden and Germany, i.e. countries that are welfare states *and* accept large refugee inflows *and* refuse to discriminate against immigrants in the provision of social services.

The other, more global, threat is one that is moving toward all developed countries, whether they have large or minimal government budgets. The accelerated aging of the adult population in all OECD countries means a strain on planning for old age, with or without the reliance on tax-based pensions and long-term care. The Nordic welfare states, like the United States since the 1980s, are world leaders that have already begun doing their social homework to deal with the rising share of the elderly.

References

AARP. 2017. Politics and Aging Fact Sheet. https://assets.aarp.org/www.aarp.org_/articles/.

Agell, Jonas, T. Lindh, and H. Ohlsson. 1999. "Growth and the Public Sector: A Reply." *European Journal of Political Economy* 15: 359–366.

Alesina, Alberto, Armando Miano, and Stefanie Stantcheva. 2018. "Immigration and Redistribution." NBER Working Paper No. 24733 (July).

Baldwin, Peter. 1990. *The Politics of Social Solidarity and the Bourgeois Basis of the European Welfare State, 1875–1975*. Cambridge: Cambridge University Press.

Bakija, Jon, Lane Kenworthy, Peter Lindert, and Jeffrey Madrick. 2016. *How Big Should Our Government Be?* Berkeley: University of California Press.

Blau, Francine. 2012. *The Economics of Women, Men, and Work*, 6th edition. Englewood Cliffs, NJ: Prentice-Hall.

Boeri, Tito. 2010. "Immigration to the Land of Redistribution." *Economica* 77, 308 (October): 651–687.

Boubtane, Ekrame, Jean-Christophe Dumont, and Cristophe Rault. 2015. "Immigration and Economic Growth in the OECD Countries 1986–2006." CESifo Working Paper Series No. 5392.

Burn-Murdoch, John. 2017. "Youth Turnout at General Election Highest in 25 Years, Data Show." *Financial Times*, June 19.

Carneiro, Pedro and James Heckman. 2003. "Human Capital Policy." In James Heckman and Anne Krueger (eds.), *Inequality in America: What Role for Human Capital Policies?* Cambridge, MA: MIT Press.

Castle, Francis G. and Steve Dowrick. 1990. "The Impact of government Spending Levels on Medium-term Economic Growth in the OECD, 1960–1985." *Journal of Theoretical Politics* 2: 173–204.

Commander, Simon, Hamid R. Davoodi, and Une J. Lee. 1997. "The Causes of Government and the Consequences for Growth and Well-Being." World Bank Policy Research Working Paper 1785. World Bank (June).

Costa, Dora L. 1998. *The Evolution of Retirement: An American Economic History, 1880- 1990*. Chicago: University of Chicago Press.

Cutler, David M. and Dan P. Ly. 2011. "The (Paper)Work of Medicine: Understanding International Medical Costs." Journal of Economic Perspectives 25, 2 (Spring): 3–25.

de la Maisonneuve, Christine, and Joaquim Oliveira Martins. 2013. "Public Spending on Health and Long-term Care: A New Set of Projections." OECD Economic Policy Papers No. 6.

Dustmann, Christian and Ian P. Preston. 2007. "Racial and Economic Factors in Attitudes to Immigration." *Berkeley Electronic Journal of Economic Analysis & Policy* 7, 1, Advances, Article 62.

Easterly, William and Sergio Rebelo. 1993. "Fiscal Policy and Economic Growth." *Journal of Monetary Economics* 32: 417–458.

Edebalk, Gunnar. 2010. "Ways of Funding and Organizing Elderly Care in Sweden." In Tommy Bengtsson (ed.), *Population Ageing: A Threat to the Welfare State?* Berlin and Heidelberg: Springer-Verlag, pp. 65–80.

Eggleston, Karen N. and Victor R. Fuchs. 2012. "The New Demographic Transition; Most Gains in Life Expectancy Now Realized Late in Life." *Journal of Economic Perspectives* 26, 3 (summer): 137–156.

Fölster, S. and M. Henrekson. 1998. "Growth and the Public Sector: A Critique of the Critics." *European Journal of Political Economy* 15 (June): 337–358.

Garfinkel, Irwin, Lee Rainwater, and Timothy M. Smeeding. 2010. *Wealth and Welfare States: Is America a Laggard or Leader?* Oxford: Oxford University Press.

Gemmell, Norman, Richard Kneller and Ismael Sanz. 2011. "The Timing and Persistence of Fiscal Policy Impacts on Growth: Evidence from OECD Countries." *Economic Journal* 121 (February): F33–F58.

Hansson, P. and M Henrekson. 1994. "A New Framework for Testing the Effects of Government Spending on Growth and Productivity." *Public Choice* 81, 3–4 (December): 381–401.

Hoynes, Hilary and Diane Whitmore Schanzenbach. 2018. "Safety Net Investments in Children." NBER Working Paper 24594 (May).

Kato, Junko. 2003. *Regressive Taxation and the Welfare State: Path Dependence and Policy Diffusion.* Cambridge: Cambridge University Press.

Korpi, Walter. 1985. "Economic Growth and the Welfare System: Leaky Bucket or Irrigation System?" *European Sociological Review* 1: 97–118.

Kotlikoff, Laurence J. and Christian Hagist. 2005. "Who's Going Broke? Comparing Healthcare Costs in Ten OECD Countries." NBER Working Paper 11833 (December).

Kneller, Richard, Michael Bleaney, and Norman Gemmell. 1999. "Fiscal Policy and Growth: Evidence from OECD Countries." *Journal of Public Economics* 74, 2 (November): 171–190.

Knuse, Agneta. 2010. "A Stable Pension System: The Eighth Wonder." In Tommy Bengtsson (ed.), *Population Ageing: A Threat to the Welfare State?* Berlin and Heidelberg: Springer-Verlag, pp. 47–64.

Landau, Daniel L. 1985. "Government Expenditure and Economic Growth in the Developed Countries." *Public Choice* 47, 3: 459–478.

Lee, Ronald D. and Timothy Miller, 2000. "Immigration, Social Security, and Broader Fiscal Impacts." *American Economic Review* 90, 2 (May): 350–354.

Lindert, Peter H. 1994. "The Rise of Social Spending, 1880–1930." *Explorations in Economic History* 31, 1 (January): 1–37.

Lindert, Peter H. 2004. *Growing Public: Social Spending and Economic Growth since the Eighteenth Century. Two volumes.* Cambridge: Cambridge University Press.

Lindert, Peter H. 2017. "The Rise and Future of Progressive Redistribution." Commitment to Equity (CEQ) Institute, Tulane University, Working Paper 73 (October). An earlier version was presented as the Fifth Angus Maddison Lecture, OECD, Paris, 4 October 2017.

Lynch, Julia. 2001. "The Age-Orientation of Social Policy Regimes in OECD Countries." *Journal of Social Policy* 30, 3: 411–436.

Lynch, Julia. 2006. *Age in the Welfare State.* Cambridge: Cambridge University Press.

McCallum, John and André Blais. 1987. "Government, Special Interest Groups, and Economic Growth." *Public Choice* 54, 1: 3–18.

Mendoza, Enrique G., Gian Maria Milesi-Ferretti, and Patrick Asea. 1997. "On the Ineffectiveness of Tax Policy in Altering Long-Run Growth: Harberger's Superneutrality Conjecture." *Journal of Public Economics* 66, 1 (October): 99–126.

Migration Advisory Committee, United Kingdom. 2018. EEA Migration into the UK: Final Report (September). https://assets.publishing.service.gov.uk /government/uploads/system/uploads/attachment_data/file/741926/ Final_EEA_report.PDF .

Nozaki, Masahiro, Kenichiro Kashiwase, and Ikuo Saito. 2014. "Health Spending in Japan: Macro-Fiscal Implications and Reform Options." IMF Working Paper WP/14/142 (August).

Organisation for Economic Cooperation and Development (OECD). 1985. *Social Expenditure 1960–1990.* Paris: OECD.

OECD. 2008. *Growing Unequal? Income Distribution and Poverty in OECD Countries.* Paris: OECD.

OECD. 2013. *International Migration Outlook 2013.* Paris: OECD.

OECD. 2018. "The Future of Social Protection: What Works for Non-Standard Workers?" Policy Brief on the Future of Work (May). www.oecd.org/employ ment/future-of-work.htm.

OECD, forthcoming. *The Future of Social Protection: What Works for Non-Standard Workers?* Paris: OECD.

Peri, Giovanni. 2016. "Immigrants, Productivity, and Labor Markets." *Journal of Economic Perspectives* 30, 4 (Fall): 1–30.

Persson, Torsten and Guido Tabellini. 1994. "Is Inequality Harmful for Growth?" *American Economic Review* 84, 3 (June): 600–621.

Pestieau, Pierre. 2006. *The Welfare State in the European Union: Economic and Social Perspectives*. Oxford: Oxford University Press.

Portes, Jonathan and Giuseppe Forte. 2017. "The Economic Impact of Brexit-Induced Reductions in Migration." *Oxford Review of Economic Policy* 33, Issue suppl 1 (1 March): S31–S44, as a pdf file (working paper) accessed via www.niesr.ac.uk, June 15, 2018.

Preston, Ian. 2014. "The Effect of Immigration on Public Finances." *Economic Journal* 124, 580, Feature Issue (November): F569–F592.

Psacharapoulos, George and Harry Anthony Patrinos. 2004a. "Returns to Investment in Education: A Further Update." *Education Economics* 12, 2 (August): 111–134.

Psacharapoulos, George, and Harry Anthony Patrinos. 2004b. "Human Capital and Rates of Return." In Geraint Johnes and Jill Johnes (eds.), *International Handbook on the Economics of Education*. Cheltenham: Edward Elgar, pp. 1–57.

Reinhardt, Uwe E. 2000. "Health Care for the Aging Baby Boom: Lessons from Abroad." *Journal of Economic Perspectives* 14, 2 (Spring): 71–84.

Scruggs, Lyle and James Allan. 2005. "The Material Consequences of Welfare States: Benefit Generosity and Absolute Poverty in 16 OECD Countries." Luxembourg Income Study Working Paper No. 409 (April).

Slemrod, Joel and Jon Bakija. 2004. *Taxing Ourselves: A Citizen's Guide to the Debate over Taxes*. 3rd edition. Cambridge: MIT Press.

Smeeding, Timothy. 2006. "Poor People in Rich Nations: The United States in Comparative Perspective." *Journal of Economic Perspectives* 20, 1 (Winter): 69–90.

Smith, Adam. 1766. *Lectures on Jurisprudence*. Edited by R. L. Meek, D. D. Raphael, and P.G. Stein. Oxford: Clarendon Press (1978).

Solijonov, Abdurashid. 2016. *Voter Turnout Trends around the World*. Stockholm: International Institute for Democracy and Electoral Assistance.

Starr, Paul. 1982. *The Social Transformation of American Medicine*. New York: Basic Books.

Thomasson, Melissa A. 2002. "From Sickness to Health: The Twentieth Century Development of U.S. Health Insurance." *Explorations in Economic History* 39, 3: 233–253.

Thomasson, Melissa A. 2003. "The Importance of Group Coverage: How Tax Policy Shaped U.S. Health Insurance." *American Economic Review*, 93, 4 (September), 1373–1384.

United States Centers for Medicare and Medicaid Services. 2012. www.cms .gov/Research-Statistics-Data-and-Systems/Statistics-Trends-and-Reports /NationalHealthExpendData/Age-and-Gender.html, accessed May 30, 2018.

United States Elections Project. Ongoing. www.electproject.org/home/voter-turnout/demographics.

Wadsworth, Jonathan, Swati Dhingra, Gianmarco Ottaviano, and John Van Reenen. 2016. "Brexit and the Impact of Immigration on the UK." Brexit Analysis No. 5, Centre for Economic Performance. http://cep.lse.ac.uk/pubs/download/brexit05.pdf.

Wang, Chen, Koen Caminada, and Kees Goudswaard. 2012. "The Redistributive Effect of Social Transfer Programmes and Taxes: A Decomposition across Countries." *International Social Security Review* 65, 3: 27–48.

Weede, Erich. 1991. "The Impact of State Power on Economic Growth Rates in OECD Countries." *Quality and Quantity* 25, 4 (November): 421–438.

Woodlander, Steffie, Terry Campbell, and David U. Himmelstein. 2003. "Costs of Health Care Administration in the United States and Canada." *New England Journal of Medicine* 349, 8 (August 21): 768–775.

Wolfinger, Raymond E. and Steven J. Rosenstone. 1980. *Who Votes?* New Haven: Yale University Press.

Cambridge Elements ☰

Public Economics

Robin Boadway
Queen's University

Robin Boadway is Emeritus Professor of Economics at Queen's University. His main research interests are in public economics, welfare economics and fiscal federalism.

Frank A. Cowell
The London School of Economics and Political Science

Frank A. Cowell is Professor of Economics at the London School of Economics. His main research interests are in inequality, mobility and the distribution of income and wealth.

Massimo Florio
University of Milan

Massimo Florio is Professor of Public Economics at the University of Milan. His main interests are in cost-benefit analysis, regional policy, privatization, public enterprise, network industries and the socio-economic impact of research infrastructures.

About the series

The Cambridge Elements of Public Economics provides authoritative and up-to-date reviews of core topics and recent developments in the field. It includes state-of-the-art contributions on all areas in the field. The editors are particularly interested in the new frontiers of quantitative methods in public economics, experimental approaches, behavioral public finance, empirical and theoretical analysis of the quality of government and institutions.

Cambridge Elements $\overline{\overline{}}$

Public Economics

Elements in the series

Cost–Benefit Analysis
Per-Olav Johansson and Bengt Kriström

Real and Imagined Threats to the Welfare State
Peter H. Lindert

A full series listing is available at: www.cambridge.org/ElePubEcon

Printed in the United States
By Bookmasters